Some people think I'm misled
for not treating my bees.
They get slimed out & full of mites,
and some become diseased.
These things exist I know it's true,
but I can't fight them all.
I do not want to be at war with life,
but life cohesively with all.

The bees have been my teachers
and they have taught me well.
To trust my intuition and listen to myself.
As I observe the things they do
I see another way.
What's right for me, might not be for you
and that will be okay.

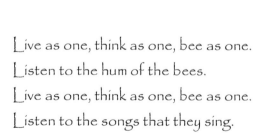

A honeybee once told me
to reconcile the past
to make changes in my future,
to help them on their quest.
They have lost their independence
and need it to survive
I will keep my bees treatment-free
and never compromise.

Live as one, think as one, bee as one.
Listen to the hum of the bees.
Live as one, think as one, bee as one.
Listen to the songs that they sing.

TABLE OF CONTENTS:

BEE BLESSED

ALOHA!

This book is dedicated to all who love wild creatures and wild places.

The purpose of this book is to provide an understanding of the nature of keeping bees in the tropics. Over the last five years I have been observing honeybees and managing a range of top bar, langstroth, and warre style hives.

As a honeybee provider for the community, it is important to me that people buying bees from me have the knowledge to keep their bees healthy. I encourage people to seek as much information about bees as possible, and attend workshops held by myself and other beekeepers to get an understanding of the choices and responsibilities that come with keeping bees.

There is no one right way.

You will create your own way, and it will be right for you.

If used correctly this manual may be used to avoid possible losses and unnecessary manipulations.

It is important to remember that some of the best lessons are learned through trial and error. Let the bees be your guide, follow your intuition and all will bee well.

This book provides information about keeping bees in the tropical environment of the east side of Hawaii. The author/publisher assumes no responsibility, legal or otherwise, for injuries, damages, or losses which may be claimed or incurred as a result, directly or indirectly, from using the information in this publication.

Design and layout by Jen Rasmussen
Photos by Jen Rasmussen, Simon Whalen, Robert Kent, Brandon Fernandez-Thompson, Joel Krueger, Pure Bliss, Zachary Augustin, and Fattah unless otherwise stated. Some public access photos are used and sources are referenced for educational purposes. These photos were researched and qualify under the fair  trade agreement.

There are several books available about bees and many of them are more informative than this book. It is not my goal to repeat what they have said. I simply want to create an understanding about bees and their hive functions for the beginning beekeeper to get started. My focus is primarily on treatment-free beekeeping in the tropics. Here on the east side of Hawaii our unique environment provides bee forage year round and we never have to feed our bees. We have heavy rainfall, summer droughts, and an environment that encourages life. Please review the references in the back of the book for other sources of useful bee information. Remember that there is no one right way. Everyone will tell you theirs and it is up to you to create your own style and beliefs that will help you evolve as a bee guardian.

A swarm of bees that was shaken into a top bar nuc box.

A queen excluder is used to cover the entrance and prohibit the queen from leaving. This method is very effective in swarm rescue and hive relocation. More on page 68.

Honeybees are not native to the Big Island of Hawaii. They were brought here to help with pollination, and of course for their honey. Hawaii is a utopia of exotic nectars and fruits. Some types of honey produced in Hawaii can only be found here. Before man came to the islands the only way foreign plants, animals, & insects could get here was by sea or air. As humans migrated here in boats and planes many new species have come to inhabit the islands, and evolve in this lush paradise.

Hawaiian honeybees had little stress in the past. Their worst predators were wax moths, mice, and rats. In 2008, the varroa destructor, a parasitic mite that feeds on honeybees made its way onto the island.

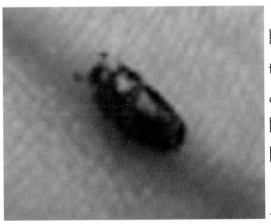

Soon after, in April 2010, the small hive beetles were found in Panaewa. Since their discovery they have spread quickly and can be found on most of the island. Recently, they were found on other Hawaiian islands.

As if that wasn't enough for the bees to cope with, they were threatened again with *Nosema Ceranae*. Nosema are spore forming bacteria that feed on the abdomens of honeybees. Bees weakened by these pests began to develop diseases of the brood (baby bees ranging from eggs to capped larvae) such as crippled wing virus and chalk brood. The bees took a major hit from the sudden attack and many died off. Others, began to adapt to the new conditions.

I began keeping bees in 2008, just before the varroa mite arrived in Hawaii. I started by reading some books and opening two hives that lived on our land. I became fascinated by them and began caring for other hives in our community. Before long, I was managing forty hives for friends and neighbors.

When varroa mites were found, a product was offered to help with mite control called Mite Away Quick Strips. MAQS are formic acid pads used in the brood nest (bee nursery) for killing mites and are approved for certified organic honey producers. I used this before the beetles arrived and observed no adverse effects on the bees. When the small hive beetle invasion began, the formic acid only added to the problems for the bees. I observed burned brood and loss of queens; as well as an increase in beetle activity. My experiences with this left me searching for alternative solutions.

Some bee specialists recommended the use of stronger miticides that seem to have less effects on the bees, but are toxic and honey stores must be removed. I chose not to take that path as well. At the end of 2011, I was down to four hives, two of them being the hives on our land. I began working with top bar hives with screened oil trays below them and had great results. A friend of mine offered me work trade for bees and I earned three shaken swarms. I was able to expand my apiary by catching their swarms and making splits from their queen cells.

I am entering 2014 with 70 hives all treatment-free and strong. I experiment with many styles of boxes, allowing bees to make all their own wax combs.

Bees know best.
Let them build their combs,
the way they choose.

Many things that I have learned about bees has been through trial and error. They are our teachers and they are not always forgiving when we mess up. Making mistakes is how we often learn how to do it right. The bees have taught me patience and empathy . I have been scolded by strong hives, only to have the same bees licking honey off my stings later.

Many people are afraid of bee stings and believe bees to be aggressive. I have experienced quite the opposite reaction from honeybees. I find them to be very calm and passive, but curious and attentive. They are very task-oriented, and are not easily distracted. Bees also pinch or bite with their mandibles. This happens more with bees who have already used their stingers.

When learning how to listen and work with bees it is best to protect oneself from stings. There are many bee companies selling protective clothing including bee suits. Most of my students wear long-sleeve white shirts, pants, veils and helmets. Gloves are also helpful although they limit one's dexterity. After working with bees for six years, I am the most comfortable and effective not wearing protective clothing.

Over time I have learned to relax around bees and not react to them flying towards me. This takes practice and the will to take a sting sometimes. The most important thing to remember is to stay calm and think clearly. Most mishaps occur when we are anxious about something.

I believe that the energy we create and what we choose to do with it directly effects our interactions with life. I have experienced this in the presence of honeybees. They are very humbling at times. I receive these lessons as opportunities to see & hear them more closely.

Breathe deep and let the bees be your guide.

BEE BASICS

There are three types of bees living in a hive. They are the queen, workers, and drones. The queen is the mother, the workers are her infertile daughters, and the drones are the males.

QUEEN BEE

Each bee starts out as an egg. The queen is the only bee that lays eggs. She determines the sex of every bee and controls the fate of the entire hive. There is usually only one queen per hive. She may live up to four years. The queen only leaves the hive to swarm, mate, or abscond (page 25).

A queen lays twice her body weight in eggs each day. Each egg is fed royal jelly, a substance made by worker bees. Only the queen eats solely royal jelly her entire life. Queens are raised in cells that look like peanuts and hang downward on the combs. Queen cells vary in size and have different appearances depending on the age of the egg/larva used and age of the wax.

All queen cells start out as little wax cups upside down on the comb. Queen cells are usually located on the side or bottom of the comb. Queen cells located on the center of the comb about mid-way up are super-sedure cells. Bees make these queens when they are replacing their existing queen. They will do this either because she is no longer releasing enough pheromones or she is not laying healthy eggs.

Bees continue to complete the queen cells as the larval stage begins on day four. On days seven through nine a cocoon is formed and the cell is completed with a thick wax coating. The queen will mature in the cell for ten to fifteen days. Here in Hawaii, queens often emerge in ten to twelve days.

It is my observation that a thin papery cap is exposed over the bottom of the cell as the queen prepares to emerge. A hive is only as strong as it's queen. However, it takes many bees to make the hive functional and sustainable.

Workers are fed bee bread, (a mixture of pollen and nectar), after the egg hatches between days three and four.

WORKER BEES

The larvae mature curled up in their cells for five days. This phase is called "uncapped brood". The larvae change direction in the cell and form a cocoon on the tenth day, and are capped over with a papery wax. This phase is called "capped brood". Capped worker brood is concave or flat on the comb. Worker bees will emerge from their cells on the twenty-first day.

The majority of bees in a hive are worker bees. The workers are the infertile females. They earn their name from the moment they are born. Workers will complete a cycle of all hive duties in thirty-five to forty-five days.

Every worker bee chews her way out of her cell and cleans it for the next egg to be laid. She begins her tasks by cleaning and warming the brood for the first two days. She then begins feeding older larvae on days three to five, and then feeds the younger brood from days six to eleven.

The next five days are spent making wax, building combs, and transporting food inside the hive. On days eighteen to twenty-one, she will guard the hive at the entrance and any other openings that might allow intruders like small hive beetles to enter the hive.

Guard bees also defend the hive on the inside by jailing beetles in propolis prisons and creating bee barriers in the corners.

The rest of their lives will be spent foraging for pollen, nectar, propolis, and water. After four to six weeks the worker bee dies.

The birth of a worker bee.

Drones are also fed bee bread when the egg hatches between days three to five. They develop the same as worker brood, except that their cells are larger and capping is convex due to the large size of the drone body. Drones are in the cocoon stage from the 10th-23rd days. They emerge on the 24th day. They are assisted in the birthing process by worker bees.

The drones are the only males in the hive. They have large compound eyes, used to sight the queen in flight. They live to mate and die when they do.

Drones spend their days hanging out in congregation areas in the sky, waiting for a queen to mate with. By dusk they return to the hive. The drones do not carry out household tasks in the hive. Their only purpose is to mate with a queen of another hive.

HONEYBEE BIOLOGY

Honeybees have a head, thorax, and abdomen. They have six legs and four wings. They have a proboscis for drinking nectar, storing and processing honey, feeding other bees and brood, and cleaning. All bees have five eyes. (This may be seen on page 15.)

OCELLI

Three of them we may not see. These are called the ocelli. The ocelli are very small and are located on the very top of the head above the compound eyes in the form of a triangle. These eyes assist bees with sun orientation so they can navigate well during the day. This is how they know when it is about to rain or when they need to return from the field before dusk.

The most obvious eyes are the compound eyes. They are large, black and centered on the head. They are made up of hundreds of single lenses called ommatidia, or retinal facets, arranged next to each other, each with its own lens and each looking in a different direction. These facets are an eight petal flower inside of a hexagon. Bees see everything in ultra-violet.

Single Retinal Facet

POLLEN

When bees collect pollen from plants they store it on their hind legs in their pollen baskets. These baskets have little hairs on them that keep the pollen from falling off. Pollen is the bees protein source.

On it's own pollen is actually not digestible, the bees cover the pollen

with nectar in the cells to utilize the enzymes. The mixture of pollen and nectar together make bee bread. Bee bread is the main food source for the young larvae, worker bees, and drones. Pollen comb is a delicious treat. To preserve freshness store in a sealed container immediately. Wax moths and small hive beetles will lay eggs on the comb while it is in the hive.

To kill any possible eggs place pollen and honey comb in the freezer for 24 hours. It is best to store pollen in a refrigerator to stop the fermentation process.

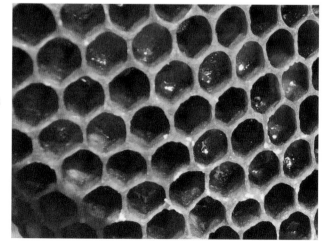

Nectar is the sweet liquid that bees get from flowers. Nectar contains water, sucrose, glucose, and fructose. The composition of these vary depending on the floral source.

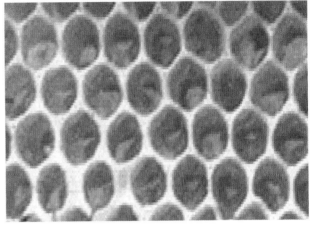

Bees use nectar for energy, it is their carbohydrate. Honeybees drink nectar through their proboscis like a straw and store it in their stomach as they transport it back to the hive. Once in the hive the bees will regurgitate the nectar into individual cells. Each cell must be stirred with the bee's proboscis and fanned with their wings to evaporate the water content.

Nectar will naturally ferment if the water is not removed. After all the stirring and fanning the resulting product is pure honey. To preserve the honey the bees cover it with a thin wax cap.

When honey is fully capped as in the picture on the left it is ready for harvest. To remove the bees use a brush, feather, fern, or hand. More on processing honey on page 70.

Many people enjoy eating comb honey. Pests may lay eggs on the comb. To preserve freshness store in a sealed container immediately and/or cover with honey.

BEE STINGS

While none of us wake up and say "I am going to get stung today", when working with bees it is likely to happen. I have weeks when I get stung every day. I have developed a tolerance to bee stings. That does not mean that it does not hurt when I get stung. Many people attend my workshops and then try to work with bees without protection. I strongly advise against this. It takes time to build a relationship and self-confidence when working with honeybees.

Because everyone's reaction is different it is important to research the options available to prevent an allergic reaction. Benadryl is the most common antihistamine that I offer to people who are having minor allergic reactions. I have yet to need something stronger. For those who may have allergies to bee stings another option is the Epi-Pen. This must be prescribed by a doctor and can be fairly expensive. The main medicine in the Epi-Pen is epinephrine, also known as adrenaline. It is best to consult a health care provider about your options regarding allergies to bee stings.

To remove a stinger use a card or finger nail and slide the stinger out the way it was inserted. Try not to puncture the sac of the stinger, this will release the venom into the body. If a part of the stinger should break off in the skin it may be removed with tweezers, though I have seldom had luck with this. A homeopathic option to relieve irritation and itching is called SSSting Stop. Applied topically this may soothe the skin and also masks the scent of the sting, which helps keep more bees from stinging. Picture on page 75.

For more information about the biology and reproductive process of honeybees I strongly recommend reading the" Biology of the honeybee" by Mark Winston. It is one of my favorite books.

GETTING STARTED

When buying a hive or catching a swarm of bees it is important to consider the kind of hive you want to work with. There is a wide range of information available on the internet about hive designs and plans to build them, as well as information about how they are working for the beekeepers who use them.

After doing my research, I chose to build a top bar hive that I found plans for on biobees.com. I made a few modifications to the design to make it work for me. I created a bottom drawer that is screened off from the bees and allows beetles to fall down into a tray.

I continue to experiment with new designs and other things to use in the trays. Some people I know are using vegetable oil, soapy water, and mineral oil. I have chosen to go with diatomaceous earth at this time because it is food grade, and I can feed the contents in the trays to my chickens and mix it into our compost.

I also work with foundation-less frame Langstroth hives. These are the traditional boxes most people think of when they picture bees. These hives are easy to work and have the capacity to produce lots of harvestable honey. The main difference in hive designs is the way you have to work them. I have heard the arguments for top bar hives and langstroth hives. I believe that it is not about the box you place them in, but how you care for them. I will briefly discuss the differences between these hives and how I have been maintaining them treatment- free.

6 frame Langstroth Hive Redesigned for easier lifting.

TOP BAR HIVES

I often encourage people to start out with the top bar hive. I like the top bar hive because it allows most of the hive to continue with its activities undisturbed. Since only one bar is removed at a time, only 2-3 sides of comb are exposed at once. To inspect the hive you start on one end, and one at a time check each comb as you work to the other side.

Bees tend to build their brood combs near the entrance on one side and honey stores on the other. I give bees a guide comb when starting new hives and place it near the entrance. It is best to place one empty bar against the side wall and then the guide comb next to it. This makes inspections easier in the future if you need to enter on the brood side. Bees often successfully jail the beetles on the end comb and edge of the bars.

Bees have adapted to a cyclic swarming pattern here. (Cycles & Swarming, page 36) You can count the days on a calendar that a shaken swarm will be preparing to swarm again in 6-8 weeks. You can visibly see evidence of this when inspecting the hive by looking for queen cups. They tend to start making the cups around week 6.

Most of the hives I care for build up very quickly. They may fill a 3' box up with honey and brood in one month. More than once, I have harvested a five gallon bucket of honey combs from one top bar hive.

Top bar hives are fun to work, easy to build, and allow bees to make their own wax combs aiding in pest & disease prevention. Best of all, they can be built to your height and never moved from the desired location.

Less heavy lifting is always better. Bees and honey can be very heavy.

It is important when working with any hive design to remember how the combs are arranged before you disturb them. The hive is an intricate puzzle. The bees create their nest to allow room for bees to travel freely between each comb/frame.

Here in Hawaii, since the small hive beetle invasion, we need to be cautious not to allow combs to touch. Mashed together combs create a space where bees can not clean and beetles will burrow in and lay eggs. I have watched healthy hives get slimed out by beetles in three days due to two combs squished together. (Read page 28 for more about small hive beetles.) It may be helpful to mark the top bars to remember what direction they were removed.

The combs in the hive are made from wax secreted from the abdomen of the bee. Each comb is made up of 100's to 1000's of cells. Each cell is a hexagon. If you look closely inside the cells, you will see a Y. The Y is also helpful in determining comb orientation. One side of the comb will have the Y upright, and the other will be turned down..

At times the bees will build off center on the frame/bar. If found early it may be fixed by cutting or bending the comb slightly. Once the bees start building crooked combs it becomes like a domino effect and makes inspections very difficult. It is best to move a straight comb to the outside of the crooked combs if the combs are full of brood. Wait to harvest crooked combs that contain brood until they are ready for a break in their brood cycle either by swarming or splitting. Bees go through continuous cycles. Entering a hive every two weeks helps prevent cross comb building.

The timing for the cycles is not always the same, but the cycle is the same. Bees start by building wax combs for the queen to lay eggs and to store nectar and pollen. Once the queen begins laying, the brood begins it's cycle. Bees will raise several generations in these combs.

As the combs age and darken the bees start to store mostly pollen, nectar, or honey in the cells. I remove the combs between 8-12 months after they are made. I find that this helps keep the hive hygienic and aids in disease prevention. The queen will lay in the old combs so I remove them when they are raising a new queen during a break in their brood cycle. They can also be moved to the outer edge of the brood nest towards the honey so the bees will not use them for raising brood.

It is good to place empty top bars between straight combs to guide the bees to build straight combs. This also helps with swarm prevention. When

LANGSTROTH HIVES

In 1852 Rev. Lorenzo Lorraine Langstroth patented the frame hive known today as the Langstroth hive.   This hive was a revolutionary idea because the only other removable frame hive in existence then was one made by Francis Huber, called The Leaf Hive, invented in Switzerland in 1789. This was one of the first hives to incorporate 'bee space' as well as a hive made by Johan Dzierzon and August von Berlepsch in Poland. .

After the creation of the removable frame hive many people began to take interest in caring for bees and harvesting honey. As popularity grew so did the interest in improving and standardizing hive boxes.

In 1857, Johannes Mehring invented wax foundation in Germany. In 1877, A.J. Root made large cell foundation predicting that larger bees would make more honey.

In 1888, G.M. Doolittle told of grafting in *Scientific Queen Rearing*. Later in 1891 bees began to disappear. This phenomenon was known as "May Disease" in 1891 and "Disappearing Disease" in 1896.

In 1922 many states made it illegal to keep bees in fixed comb hives such as skeps and clay pots. This led to the mass industrialization of the bee. Not long after, came artificial insemination, corn syrup, and a repeat of "disappearing disease" in 27 states and Mexico.

In 1976, bee die offs in Idaho were traced to Penncap M, a pesticide found in pollen.

In 1984, tracheal mites were found in Florida and shortly after the varroa mites arrived there too.

Why is all of this important?

In order for me to figure out how to keep bees in a way that felt right to me I had to learn what they have been through up until now.

Bees have been mistreated and abused.

They have been exposed to so many chemicals and pests over the last several decades that it is no wonder we are seeing the losses and trials they are facing now. The functionality of the Langstroth hive has enabled the use of miticides, antibiotics, and much more. It is my belief that the use of treatments cause the bees to become dependent on them and have adverse effects over long-term use like tougher mites and the need to use stronger miticides.

The Langstroth hive has its advantages and certainly provides an easily manipulated structure to house bees in. Visiting the bees every two weeks helps to develop straight combs on the frames.

CAPPED HONEY COMB

EXTRACTED HONEY COMB

I use foundation-less frames in my Langstroth hives to let the bees make all of their own combs. I remove all wax comb after one year to promote hygienic behavior and remove disease spores & contamination. I have chosen to keep these hives because so many bee-

keepers use them and have a knowledge about them. It is good when networking and offering bees to have something for everyone. I find them to be heavy, expensive, and labor intensive. I have recently started working with 6 frame boxes to help my body (pg. 18). One honey super may weigh up to 75 lbs.. The lighter the box the easier it is to lift it. Using buckets and harvesting into them helps with heavy lifting.

TOOLS & TERMINOLOGY

The hive tool- There are many different styles of these available through bee-keeping companies such as Mann Lake (HD-588), brushy mtn. bees, dadant, etc.

The Smoker- Smoke disguises the scent of pheromones. When a bee stings something it is marked with a scent. The smell is called isopentyl acetate. It is also found in bananas and pears.

Hat or Helmet- It is important to wear a hat. Getting stung on the head hurts.

Veil- Veils keep bees from stinging you in the face, they are very useful.

Bee Suit- There are many different styles of bee suits available. I have found that a long sleeve cotton button down shirt and jeans works just as well.

Brush/Feather- When you need to remove bees from combs it is good to have. Long grass and ferns work fine as well.

Buckets- Bees make different products that all need to be harvested separately. Nectar, Honey, Pollen, and Propolis. 6 buckets and a container are needed for the whole process.

Hive/Box- Many different styles are available.

Langstroth- removable frame hive
          8-10 frames per box
          deep 9 5/8" x 19"
          super 6 5/8" x 19"

Top Bar- trapezoidal hive.
          3' long, 17-21" bar

Warre-   Free form box hive~
      wild nest like a hollow tree.

Queen Cage- Plastic or wooden container with holes used for the temporary removal or introduction of the queen.

Queen Excluder- Rectangular grid screen made of metal or plastic. Used to allow workers to run freely but isolates the queen inside the hive.

Nuc- Small hive of bees, usually 3-5 combs. Approximately 3-5 lbs. of bees. Started using a queen or queen cells.
Small nuc boxes are often used when starting new hives.

Shaken Swarm- Swarm of bees shaken from an existing hive, tree, etc. approximately 3-5 lbs. of Bees and a queen.

Split- Intentional division of a hive to make a new one.

Brood Cycle- The time that an egg has been laid in a cell to the time that it emerges from a larval stage

Abscond- Bees abandon the hive due to pests, diseases, or other environmental factors.

Field Force- The forager bees returning with nectar and pollen flying around the entrance.

Nectar- Sweet substance that is produced by plants. Honeybees drink nectar and take it back to their hive where they use their proboscis to regurgitate it into cells. they use their wings and proboscis to remove the water content and turn it into honey, which they cap with wax to preserve. Nectar ferments when harvested due to the high moisture content.

PESTS & DISEASES

I have previously mentioned the pest issues we face here on the Big Island. I believe that it is best to focus on how to strengthen the body to enable it to heal itself rather than deal with symptoms of a deeper problem. It is my opinion that miticides, antibiotics, etc. all treat symptoms of a greater issue, which is weakened immune systems. We need to allow life to evolve and each living creature must learn how to defend itself and co-exist with others. The strong will survive.

Varroa destructor, the varroa mite.

Varroa will live in a hive and have very little effect on it if the hive is healthy. Strong bees who are very hygienic will remove sick brood regularly. If I find a hive that is failing from varroa infestation, I pull the queen from the hive and make a split with her in another box. I remove all excess honey

Photo from~ bees.msu.edu ~ public access

and pollen from the hive, and leave them with plenty of brood and eggs for rearing a new queen.

During the time that the queen is developing in her cell the workers are busy cleaning up the empty cells, bees are emerging from their cells and varroa mites are being released with them. The bees groom and clean all day, removing the varroa, and purifying the hive for the next brood cycle. My bees & I have evolved to a 3 month swarm/split cycle. The break in brood production is essential for the bees to properly clean their combs. Continual use of combs breeds disease. While I am aware of these cycles, I allow my bees to lead the way when making my decision to intervene. Often hives with high varroa infestations start making queen cells/cups and are already preparing to swarm.

Deformed wing virus- A symptom of high mite populations. Wings look as if they have been chewed off. This is also associated with a lack of hairs and a graying color. Early symptoms of DW are undeveloped larvae slumped in cells, partially capped dead brood, and snotty looking larvae.

Chalk Brood- A fungus. Larva dries up and looks like a small piece of chalk in the cell. Possible causes are poor ventilation, damp/moist environment, poor hygiene, or nutrition.

Picture from~ nationalbeeunit.com ~ public access images.

Slime out-

Hive overrun by small hive beetles and turned to a sticky slop of beetle larvae.

Mite Count-

Tests can be done to monitor the mite levels in a hive. The most bee friendly method is to use a sticky board with a screen over it. Bees groom themselves and the mites fall & stick to the board.

50+ mites in a 24 hour period is a high mite Count.

Nosema Ceranae-

A small, unicellular parasite. The dormant stage of nosema is a long-lived spore which is resistant to temperature extremes and dehydration. Feeds on the honeybee internally.

Picture from ~ aem.asm.org ~ public access image.

Wax Moths-

Small gray moths that eat wax and wood. They burrow through combs and leave behind a stringy web of black crumbs (poop). Picture from~ nurturing-nature.co.uk ~ public access image.

THE SMALL HIVE BEETLE

I have mentioned the tragic times that we faced in 2010 when the small hive beetles first arrived on the Big Island. I do not wish to walk down memory lane on that topic. However I do wish to educate you on the lessons I have had to learn the hard way.

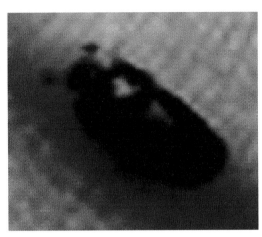

First some basic facts about the small hive beetles.

*They may fly up to 15 miles and will often be found entering a hive around dusk..

*SHB prefer pollen and brood for the high protein content. They will eat honey to create pathways to the brood and pollen. Once larvae eat and crawl through honey it turns to a fermented gooey mess.

*Larvae are attracted to the light and crawl out of the hive to pupate in the soil. They may burrow out 150 feet and 9 ft. down.

This fact alone makes products such as GARDSTAR (a ground drench made with pyrethrins that kills beetle larvae) worthless, especially in Hawaii due to the rain. Larvae may also pupate in the debris that collects on the bottom board.

I switched to screen bottom boards to help with this but I still need to maintain the beetle drawer and remove collecting debris.

*An adult SHB may lay 1000 eggs per day, and those eggs may hatch in 72 hours if the temperature is 80 degrees Fahrenheit. In Hawaii, we have the ideal environment for SHB's to hatch in 48-72 hours.

*SHB have a hard exoskeleton which protects them from the bees stings. Honeybees will fight, jail, starve, chase and carry the beetle away from the hives, but they cannot sting them.

*SHB also like fruit such as star fruit, jackfruit, papaya, guava, and mango.

Eradication of the small hive beetles is impossible.

What we do with what we know is everything. Understanding adaptation is also critical when intervening in a natural process. After losing many hives, reading lots of literature about small hive beetles, and hearing from beekeepers who had worked with SHB's, I was determined to find a way to live with these parasites.

The trouble is that, other than killing them, there is no way to stop them or prevent them from entering a hive. If killing something is your only option, the question of how to do it must be considered.

There are in-hive traps that will attract beetles to oil and they drown in it. Oil is definitely the most effective product to use to drown beetles. I have a difficult time supporting the GMO oil industry and I can not afford oil for all my hives so I have chosen diatomaceous earth. Oil traps must be changed weekly, though many beekeepers will leave them in for two weeks.

I caution against using in-hive traps because the oil may become rancid and is unhygienic for the bees, and the beetles may pile up inside the trap and use the trap as a safe haven to hide from the bees.

Many things in life are unpredictable and you may not be able to visit your bees every fourteen days. For me now keeping seventy -/+ hives I definitely do not get through them all every two weeks so I am trying to create a system that is less involved and empowers my bees to control the pests themselves.

Beetle Jail in-hive trap best used with oil and changed every 10 days. Works best with Langstroth hives.

Another option for in-hive traps. We used vegetable and mineral oil in these to attract and kill beetles. The trap Velcro's to the frame and stands upright. I found these to be labor intensive and messy. I do not recommend this trap.

I have found that they do this very well and with the aid of an under hive trap/tray I am able to reduce SHB populations, maintain the trays without having to disturb the bees and offer more area for the beetles to fall through the screen.

I mentioned before that I have tried many different solutions to drowning beetles. I am pleased with the results I am having using the diatomaceous earth. Compared with oil at $8-$13 per gallon, a 50 lb. bag of d.e. costs $36 at Del's in Hilo.

D.E. must be sifted and changed as needed. I like to remove all solid matter and shake the tray every time I visit the hive. It is best to do this down wind and away from the hive after you finish inspecting. This is important so that you do not soil the d.e. by spilling honey on it when inspecting the hive. Honey spilled into the d.e. tray will clump and provide a place for beetles to climb on and avoid the d.e..

The tray shown here is under a 1/8" mesh screen. I use disposable cake tins and use them for years. This is the most inexpensive method I have found. It is very important when working with d.e. to make sure that it does not get wet. We recently had a storm here with high winds and many covers blew off the hives. There were losses and we had some clean up to do.

Hive entrances need to be protected from wind. I have seen hives with a dusty layer of d.e. on the inside walls. It was clear that the hive was getting to much wind. After changing the position of the entrance this problem stopped.

Trays that have been saturated with honey or water become a problem rather than a solution. The d.e. clumps and makes a solid surface for beetles to walk on as well as providing them with a safe place to congregate away from the bees. The trays only work if you can maintain them properly.

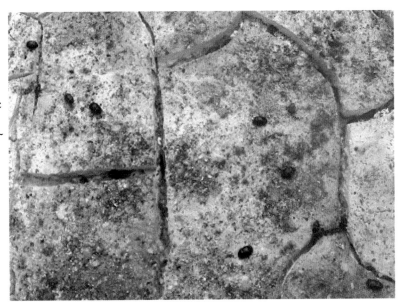

Top bar hives have a similar system for beetle control. The tray runs the length of the hive and is made of steel. These trays are custom built and are very durable and long lasting. With both hive designs it is important to clean out the tray area when changing & cleaning the tray.

Debris that builds up makes a great place for beetle larvae to pupate. Wax moths and other critters will collect in the tray area as well. On the east side of Hawaii where our hives are located we experience heavy rainfall, winds, and lots of big, fallen trees. It is not uncommon for me to find large trees blocking the roads to my yards. This makes after-storm clean up very difficult. I am continually improving my roofing designs and trying to find the best option.

I have someone build hives for me and he makes a curved roof that is leak proof and durable. I prefer these but they cost around $50 so they are not always in my budget for my expanding apiary. I have opted recently to light weight siding that I can purchase at Home Depot for $15 and divide it into two covers. This is the most economical option but it is hard to weigh down.

We have lots of rocks around the yards so all of my hives are covered with metal or plastic roofing/siding pieces and rocks. I also use cinder blocks when they are available.

After reading Wyatt Mangum's book called Top Bar Beekeeping: Wisdom and Pleasure Combined, I have been tying down my covers with rope and securing them the way he describes. I recommend reading his book to get ideas on other styles of top bar hives and management practices. Remember when reading book on mainland beekeeping that hive management in the tropics differs considerably.

There are many factors to consider when dealing with the small hive beetles. Try not to focus on the problems, but pay attention to the details and create the solution. Bees guard beetles in propolis traps by themselves. This may be seen in all of my hives. When we open the lid to the hive or remove the top bars from the edges we release the beetles from those guarded areas because the bees become frantic due to our intrusion and often the use of a smoker. I use very little smoke for this reason. The smoker is used more to mask the scent of stings than to manipulate the bees. When the beetles run free from their bee enforced jails I squish them.

Bee-made propolis prison.
The beetles shown in this picture are dead. They were surrounded by bees and starved.

I have witnessed other beekeepers use smoke to get beetles to run up to the top of the hive. I actually believe this to be counterproductive because the bees end up chasing the beetles around the combs and the beetles find new places to hide from them. This distraction from their normal tasks and extra chaos lowers the productivity of the hive and when they become agitated they release an alarm pheromone. That pheromone actually attracts more beetles to the hive.

This is why we are starting to see bees hanging on the outside of the boxes more frequently. These bee gauntlets are their solution for beetle control. Strength in numbers is a great strategy. The hive in the picture looks like it is about to swarm. However, the hive actually only has two frames of brood and a queen. There are approximately five lbs. of bees in the hive, most of them being workers. Under the roof edge there is a cluster of bees trapping beetles under the lip of the lid. At the entrance they cover it like a carpet and trap the beetles in the corners of the box.

Two years ago if I would have seen this when entering my apiary I would have thought that the bees were outgrowing their box and needed more room. Upon further observations, I realized that more room would be devastating for these bees. **It is important to have enough bees in the hive for one bee per square inch of comb on all the combs.** Empty frames with holes and gaps provide places for beetles to hide. It is important that there are enough bees to trap and guard the beetles.

Beekeeping in Hawaii has changed forever due to the varroa mites and small hive beetles. While these changes create more work and complications, they also create better bee guardians and awareness. My bees continue to teach me patience and perseverance daily. That is why this book continues to evolve and will never truly be finished!

I have been observing over the last five years changes in the behavior of the bees. While genetics certainly have something to do with hive vitality, I have witnessed a change in the bees reproductive cycle which appears to revolve around varroa infestations. I will explain more about that on the next page.

The most important part of the whole experience is to remember that the bees know best. If they are choosing to swarm eight weeks after the last swarm, they must need to do it. You may choose to split it or catch the swarm, but trust the bees to do what is right for them.

You may read the last paragraph and then later read contradicting information when I discuss swarms and reproduction. The population of the hive at the time they are choosing to swarm is a determining factor in choosing to stop bees from swarming. I make my decision to split or not by checking the brood, population of bees, health of the brood and combs, and the size of the box they are in. Depending on the conditions of the hive I may remove the queen and allow the bees to make another or remove the queen cells and combs they are on and place a queen excluder over the entrance of the hive. This gives the bees time to recover and the beekeeper time to observe their development.

Cycles & Natural Prevention

I have monitored many hives in wild conditions and warre style box hives where bees are allowed to build fixed combs that can not be inspected. By observing these hives I have discovered several cycles that bees use to help control pests. The most important factors in these cycles is the timing and the amount of combs that the bees have built. By observing your bees natural cycles you may begin to understand the differences in your hives. Although many of the cycles are similar they actually vary considerably depending on overall hive strength and hygiene. For example, many people believe that if a hive swarms they have out grown their hive and are ready to multiply.

Here in Hawaii we see new hives that after 8 weeks swarm when they are not strong enough to multiply. When considering this unusual phenomenon I began to notice that these young hives are also very attractive to small hive beetles and varroa mites. The bees are using their ability to swarm to create a pause in brood production and allow the worker bees to clean up the combs. This process is quite brilliant and the bees figured it out all by themselves. Most of what I do for small hive beetles is prevention. The trays are helpful in controlling the population growth but the goal is for bees to limit their growth independently. Beetles are the most problematic after a hive is split or swarms due to the decreased population of bees and uncovered combs.

The trouble with the premature swarming is that the hive seldom builds up enough to properly feed the brood. This results in malnourished workers and underfed small queens. These hives tend to go through one or two brood cycles with the new queen before beginning super-sedure cells and replacing her with a new well-fed queen.

You may identify the difference in these cells by their size and shape. A healthy queen cell should look like the one in the picture on page 36. Bees will make many cells at a time and may even swarm multiple times. It is important to monitor your bees at times of swarming to prevent over-swarming.

I have noticed some hives will "swarm to death". This is rare but has definitely happened. Symptoms of a hive that may be genetically challenged in this area are poor hygiene, slow production, uncovered combs, underfed queens, and excessive drone populations. If caught early these hives may be saved by giving them queen cells from a strong hive that are 5-8 days old or a queen in a cage with attendants.

If using a cell you will want to be sure to remove other cells before inserting your new cell. Be sure to do the same if using a queen as well, but you will also need to attach the cage to a frame or top bar with a rubber band and then release her in two days. When releasing the queen it is important to monitor the bees reaction to her. If the bees are balling her cage, wait to release her. I like to use a hydrosol spray made by The Queen Bee Project called "Bee Friendly". This is best used when combining bees or introducing a new queen to a hive.

To help clarify the cycles I will give a summary of the timeline for healthy hive cleansing and reproduction. It is important when working in these cycles to remember that not all hives are created equally. They have their own personality, hygienic practices, and construction styles. Think outside the box and work with your bees as they show you who they are.

The cycles explained here are just guidelines for healthy treatment-free management practices.

•6-8 week cycle-   Bees tend to begin making queen cups/cells at this stage and preparing to swarm. I remove the cups/cells and drop empty frames/bars between the straight ones.

Once I have found cups/cells I will inspect again in 7-14 days to see if the bees have taken my advice or if they have continued to raise a new queen. When the old queen leaves a hive about 75% of the bees in the hive will follow her. At this stage of development the hive is not often strong enough to support such a loss.

•   3 month cycle-   Assuming that the bees did not swarm at the 6-8 week period you will want to support them in their decision to swarm at this point in time.

I do not have time to catch all the swarms that I have so I intervene at this time and make a split by removing the queen and 3-5 lbs. of bees with some of their brood combs and move them to another location. It is best to move your bees 3-5 miles from their original location. If it is desired to keep them on the same property the queen must be caged or a queen excluder must be placed over the entrance. The hive must be facing a different direction and have some distance from the original hive. I plug the entrance of the hive for 12 to 24 hours and open up the beetle drawer and remove the tray to give them ventilation. They will overheat and die if they do not have proper ventilation.

I often take the queen when making the splits so that I do not have to move them off the property. Always shake in more bees than you need when leaving bees in the same yard because many of the bees will fly back to the original location.

The bees in the original hive will make many queen cells and will still try to swarm. There are several ways to deal with this. I use the queen cells to make splits with bees from other hives to multiply my apiary. Creating many small nucs is how I am able to sell bees and maintain my number of colonies.

If you do not wish to multiply your apiary you may monitor the bees and their cell development. Place a queen excluder over the entrance of the hive for the duration of cell development and three days after expected emergence. Before removing the excluder check the hive for virgin queens. If you find only one queen remove the excluder.

If you find two queens remove one and cage her with some attendants to feed and care for her. Give her to bees that need her or find a friend who may need a queen. I do not recommend selling virgin queens. They need to survive the introduction and mating process before they are reliable.

Introducing a virgin queen to bees who had a mated queen is tricky. I often cage the queen for two days in the hive so the bees get to know her scent.

Bees will ball (surround and attack) and kill a queen who does not smell like them. It is important to cage the queen when introducing her to bees who do not know her. It is also important to make sure that the bees stay well fed while they begin building fresh white comb for her to lay eggs in right away. By the time the queen is released the bees will have made new combs for her to lay in. Do not cage a queen for more than four days. If caging a queen be sure that she has attendants to feed her and queen candy (powdered sugar & honey) to eat.

Eggs may be challenging to see at first. Especially on the white combs. Examine the picture on the right. Each cell has a Y in the middle of it. In the center of the Y is an egg.

Each egg is fed royal jelly for three days and then will develop into a larva.

Go back to pages 11-13 for more about the feeding cycles and how they affect bee biology. When looking at dark combs it may be difficult to identify the eggs as well. Turning the combs so that the sun shines behind you will help to make them more visible.

When turning combs be sure to move them in a vertical position. Turning combs horizontally could cause breakage.

The presence of eggs in the comb will tell us a lot about what is happening in the hive. For instance, if you find eggs in the comb you know that a queen was laying them within the last three days.

If you do not find a queen, eggs are visible, and queen cells are present in the hive then the queen may have swarmed within the last 48 hours. It is easy to miss the queen even when your eyes are well-trained to find her so do not be discouraged if you are unable to identify her in your inspections. I often stop my search if I do not find queen cells/cups and I find eggs. That tells me that everything is okay.

When you find more than one egg in a cell, that is another story. A healthy queen only lays one egg per cell, (with the exception of a young queen who has just mated). Laying workers will lay more than one egg in a cell and those eggs do not actually make worker bees. They will develop into diploid drones who are not fertile and can not create comb or provide food for the colony. A hive with a laying worker is lost if not re-queened and given healthy brood from another hive. My solution when I find evidence of a laying worker is to examine the combs for a bee that looks different from the rest. Sometimes she is easy to find. Often she is not. No matter if you are able to identify her or not I recommend shaking all the bees off the combs in front of another hive or location away from the original hive location. Obviously many bees will fly back. The hope is that the laying worker will not. In the original location I place the hive with brood combs, bees, a caged queen or queen cell and a comb of honey. Basically I make a split and put it in the location of the original hive to catch the field force. If you do not have an extra queen or cell available do not worry. Giving a queen-less hive eggs and brood will often be enough to fix the situation. The bees will raise a new queen from the eggs by feeding them royal jelly and building queen cups around the eggs. There must be enough brood and bees in the hive to sustain them for three weeks. That is approximately the time it takes to get from egg to mated queen.

Remember to let the bees guide you. I could write about 20 unpredictable situations I have been in from queens born with no wings to finding 7 virgin queens emerging at the same time. No matter what the scenario there is always a back up solution.

Give the bees brood, eggs, pollen, and honey and let them raise a new queen. If a hive is unable to sustain itself, let it go. I know that may seem harsh or uncaring to say that but the truth is that if a hive continues to struggle even when given all the tools they need for success then it may be time to let them go. This does not mean that you or they have failed.

Beekeeping is all about learning new things and trying out new ideas to enhance the experience for yourself and the bees. That is what makes it fun and exciting for me. Sharing what I have learned with others continues to teach me more about myself and how I choose to create my reality. There is a great story called "The Bee-Man Of Orn" written by Frank R. Stockton. In this story the bee-man is told that he has been transformed from his original self and so he embarks on a journey with his bees to find what he originally was. I wish to encourage you to read this story yourself so I will not share more about how the story ends. What I choose to share is a line from the book that

is meaningful to me. The bee-man is laying in a field and watching his bees return from the flowers laden with sweet pollen and says to himself: "They know just what they have to do, and they do it. But alas for me! I know not what I may have to do. And yet, whatever it may be, I am determined to do it."

Patience, perseverance, determination, surrender, and acceptance are some of the best gifts I have received.

Genetic Diversity

Over the last four years I have been working with four different genetic lines. These are Carniolan (*Apis mellifera carnica*), German Black Bee or European dark bee (*Apis mellifera mellifera*), Italian honeybee (*Apis mellifera ligustica*), Cordovan (*Apia mellifera* ?).

All of these have their own strengths and weaknesses. I believe that bees need genetic diversity to survive. If they do not interbreed with other kinds of bees they may not be capable of dealing as efficiently with the pests and diseases that threaten them everyday. In my hives you may see a large variance of color, size, comb construction methods, queens laying pattern, etc.

You may even see another kind of bee altogether called a Leafcutter bee. These bees roll up small ovals of leaf and create a nest on the edges of the top bars and other hidden areas.

I began to notice leaf cutter bees shortly after the decline of the honeybees in 2010. It was at this time that we saw a rise in carpenter bees, hummingbird moths, and other solitary bees I have yet to identify.

~All the freaky creatures make the beauty of the world.~

I do not believe that any one species is better than another. We are all connected. This was clear to me during the decline of the bees. I saw other pollinators stepping up and though we did see a decrease in food production on our land, we also continued to have enough food to sustain us. I give thanks to the wild pollinators for that. As I discuss more about my experiments with genetics I wish to help you fully understand the reasoning and conclusions that I have developed over the years. I will start out with a breakdown of each kind of honeybee that I am learning with and what I have witnessed in their growth.

Carniolan bee
(*Apis mellifera carnica*),
is a subspecies of the western honey bee. The Carniolan honeybee is native to Slovenia, southern Austria, and parts of Croatia, Bosnia and Herzegovina, Serbia, Hungary, Romania, and Bulgaria. I have not been able to find any information on when and how these bees were brought to Hawaii. Queen breeders have been working with these bees for a very long time here on the Big Island. I was introduced to them back in 2011 when I took a job working for another beekeeper in Puna. I worked for bees and received two hives that each had Carniolan queens. I multiplied these hives many times and now have several daughters of the original mothers.

These bees are very hygienic, produce a large amount of honey and brood in cycles, as well as swarming on cycles to clean up varroa infestations. They tend to be very calm and easy to work with.

They are very aggressive with the small hive beetles and will create beetle jails, physically attack the beetles, and fly away from the hive with them. The queens and bees differ slightly in color and size. Most are very dark with distinct amber/golden stripes. The amber/gold bee that may be seen in the picture on the previous page that stands out is the queen.

Now about half of the 50-70 hives I care for carry this lineage. My hive numbers fluctuate with the cycles and seasons. Times when nectar is more abundant the bees grow faster. I wish to maintain a maximum of 75 hives at any time. I once had 97 hives and I found I did not have time for anything but bees. Now I know what is realistic for me to keep up with and maintain properly without stress and wearing myself out. As I have learned what my desires and limitations are I have learned how to maintain a peaceful relationship with bees. I wish the same for you. Learn with them as they grow and they will teach you what you need to know.

German Black Bee (Apis mellifera mellifera),

these small, dark-colored honey bees are sometimes called the German black bee, although they originated from Britain to eastern central Europe. There are three main races, namely * mellifera (brown bee), *lehzeni (heathland bee), and *nigra (black bee). While I am not sure which it is that I work with here I know them to be very black or black and brown and slightly more

defensive than other bees against the pests and intruders.

I have found them to be quite peaceful to work with most of the time. I know them best by their brood pattern. These queens are very thorough and will lay their eggs in a spiral pattern working from the inside of the comb to the outside. These are great bees to work with and I have acquired them by removing wild hives from structures and catching swarms. I have continued to propagate them by allowing them to raise natural cell queens and making splits or catching their swarms. While most of the literature I have read says that these bees are less prone to swarming I have observed frequent swarming in cycles that appears to revolve around varroa infestations. These bees are extremely successful managing the pests and diseases on their own. I have observed a higher production of propolis prisons for beetles, corner prisons made by bees, and more aggressive chasing and harassment of the beetles.

The black bees are also more prone to retiring their darker combs to pollen and nectar after a few brood cycles. They tend to favor the lighter combs. When forced to stay on darker combs for brood production I have observed a decrease in hive health over the period of a several months. This makes sense to me because of *Nosema Ceranae*. Old combs may contain numerous spores and will overtime weaken the bees immune systems. Removing old combs within a year will help to improve hive health. Freezing old combs may help to reduce the number of spores and allow the comb to be reused. If it is your intention to re-use old combs I recommend placing them in the honey storage areas. For a top bar hive this would be several combs after the brood nest. If you are placing it in to give bees a straight comb as a guide place one empty bar between the brood and the old comb. This will help to keep the bees from connecting their combs and they will be less likely to put brood in the old comb. If you find yourself considering what to do with an aging, dark brood comb, let it go. Bees can make a full comb over night if given enough honey and pollen. They will replace the old comb with a new clean one in its place.

As beekeepers we may help the bees with 'space management'. Harvest honey and pollen when it is ready and remove the old to make room for the new.

In the wild these bees abandon their hive after multiple brood cycles and relocate to build another. I have observed this many times. The sites that I have found these bees there are many old combs and hives located near them This shows that the bees are starting over on fresh combs but staying close to the old nest. I have also found on many occasions that bees will move into an old nest and build new combs off of the old ones. For the past five years the German black bee has intrigued and amazed me as I have studied them and witnessed their adaptability, strength, and vitality.

Italian honeybee (*Apis mellifera ligustica*),

is thought to originate from the conti-
nental part of Italy, south of the Alps,
and north of Sicily. Their abdomens
have brown and yellow bands. Among
different strains of Italian bees, there are
three different colors: Leather; bright
yellow (golden); and very pale yellow
(Cordovan). Their bodies are smaller
and their over hairs shorter than those of

the darker honeybee races. Italian honeybees tend to produce lots of honey in the summer months and they have a lower tendency for swarming. I have observed more diseases related to varroa infestations with the Italian bees.

A friend of mine bought seven five-frame nucs from a beekeeper in Kona for $150 each. The bees came with brood that was on foundation started dark combs. He worked with these bees in alternative hive designs and shook most of them off of their combs and had them start over. Many of the hives built new combs and stored lots of honey in their first cycle of brood production. After their first major growth spurt he split them and multiplied the hives.

Some of the splits flew away, some slimed out, and some continued to grow strong. By the first wet season the hives started to develop deformed wing virus. I removed the queens from the hives that were making queen cells and made a split using bees from another hive. Some of the hives cleaned things up for a while.

I took over the hives for my friend and with the remaining four hives that were in my apiaries I began to do some experimentation. I took Italian queens and gave them to German bees with brood. I gave the Italian bees a comb of eggs from the German bees and they raised queen cells with the German queens' eggs. I did this in many variations with all the hives to see what would happen to the mix in their genetic lines.

What I have learned from this is that you may encourage bees to acquire or let go of certain traits that you wish to alter. This is a subtle encourage-ment and the bees are the ones who ultimately get to decide. I tried to intro-duce an Italian queen who came from a very docile hive into a large split I made with half of a German hive that was outgrowing it's box. I caged the queen with three of her own attendants and attached her to a top bar between two brood combs. I came back on day two to release the queen and the bees were very agitated. I decided to come back the next day to see if they had calmed down. They had not. I decided to release the queen, I thought maybe that would help them to relax but instead they tried to attack her immediately. I managed to get her away from them and kept her safe back in the cage. I removed her from the hive and left the bees alone.

I came back a few days later to introduce another queen to them only to find that they had already started five new queen cups and were content to make their own queen. By the time the queen cells were eight days old the hive had gone back to being quite enjoyable to work with and had definitely calmed down substantially. The Italian queen found a new home amongst some sweet Carniolan bees and eventually swarmed. The queen that was raised from her eggs were darker in color and over time I stopped being able to tell the difference between the bees. I often find many different colors or bees in the hives.

It is important to offer bees the tools they need for success but allow them to use them if they wish and accept the outcome if they do not. I no longer have pure Italian honeybees in my apiaries. I have mixed them up and combined the genetics many times to help develop a stronger bee that is capable of defending itself.

I had an interesting experience learning from a fiery Cordovan queen and her attentive workers. I acquired them from a wild hive that I removed from a shelf outside of a house.

When I was removing the hive I found no eggs, open queen cells, and one closed queen cell, all evidence that they had recently swarmed. The bottom shelf was crawling with beetle larvae.

I put the bees, the queen cell and usable combs in a Langstroth frame with rubber bands and secured the comb in place. I moved the bees in their new hive to my home apiary and put them near some bananas, a garden, a fire pit, and about 15 feet from a main trail at our house. When the bees were being removed and when they first arrived on our land they were pleasant and easy to work around. I checked them shortly after I brought them home and found that the queen cell was open but could not find the queen. I did find eggs though. I was content knowing that they had worked it out and left them alone for two weeks.

On my next inspection I received six stings in the face and neck just opening up the hive. I could not work through the box easily because they had built all their combs extra wide so that they all overlapped each other.

My trying to separate the frames sent the bees into a rage and they proceeded to sting me more. I decided to add a honey super with some recently extracted frames that had honey in them. I put three frames with comb and three empty frames alternating in the top box. I was working with a six frame box. I placed the super on top of the hive and again the bees went wild. I closed them up and left them alone for two weeks. About a week after their inspection a crew of helpers got stung pulling weeds around the garden and fire pit. There were several more experiences where the bees got very aggressive with people. Weed pulling, walking on the trail, scything the grass, or attending other hives in the area would set them off and they would sting often.

I got into the hive once more and found the queen. She was very orange-red. She moved quickly and the bees became extremely ferocious once I noticed her. I began to dread having to work with these bees. They were not very much fun to be around.

I took the queen and mixed her with some very healthy German bees. I let the fiery hive raise a new queen. The next queen continued to show the resemblance to her mother and I soon decided to split them in half. I took the queen and half of the combs and moved them to another location. The bees in the original location I gave a frame of eggs from another hive, and they raised a new queen from the eggs.

By doing this I tamed the fiery reds and eventually I sold some of them to other beekeepers. I still have a few of these Cordovan queens but I am not seeing the pure red anymore. Now they all have a black band on their abdomens. Their temperament has become much more pleasant to work with.

The information I have shared about genetic diversity is from my own experiments and observations. I have not studied in other bee yards and I have not read this in a book. I researched distinct characteristics of bees that have been found in Hawaii and these bees are the ones who matched the descriptions. I believe the more diverse the genetics become the healthier the bee.

If you are struggling with an aggressive hive my first recommendation is to re-queen them but you do not need to kill the old queen. Changes in location, sun exposure, land maintenance, etc. will alter a hives defensive characteristics. Before re-queening try changing the scenery. Pull weeds around their hive, cut the grass in the area, cut down trees that shade them in the middle of the day. These are all things that could help improve hive health without actually even opening your hive.

By working with the different bees I have collected I realize how important it is to honor each hive's individuality. Though they all go through the same roles and tasks they each have their own personality. Just as we humans do. I have a practice of positive thought that I use each time I go to the bee yard.

I do not think about getting stung,

I do not worry about what will happen later.

I take the time to get to know each hive and try to understand what their particular needs are. This has helped me develop close relationships with many of my hives.

Some hives are just known to have a less than cheery disposition. As you grow with your bees you will see changes in their behavior. These become apparent during the days prior to swarming, when they feel threatened, and if there are changes in their environment. Storms and long periods of rain may cause them to react more defensively as well. It is possible that most of the unpleasant interactions one may share with bees is directly related to the persons projections. What we think and speak we may attract to ourselves.

Enter the hive with a peaceful mind. Allow the time with the bees to be a sort of meditation. Let your body relax and remember to breathe. Keep your thoughts pleasant and your intentions clear. Listen to the sound of the hive. Smell their scent. This is a purely sweet experience.

FIXED COMB HIVES

It is important to remember that there are no right answers. The best you may hope for is to learn from your bees how to evolve with them and aid them in their evolution. As I watched my bees these last few years I have learned many lessons, many of them the hard way. Through my experimentation and watching bees grow in different hive styles I have been witness to many changes and adaptations by the bees.

I experimented with a variety of 'wild' hives last year. I used a 12" x 12" box hive where you stack the boxes 4 tall with an entrance on the bottom box. The top cover of the box was a Masonite board with holes drilled in it. Another solid board would rest on top. The board with holes is to be used later as a queen excluder when we add the honey super. Bees would build natural combs on the cover and once they were building in 3/4 boxes I would add the honey box on top.

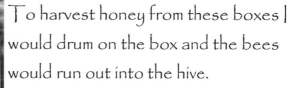

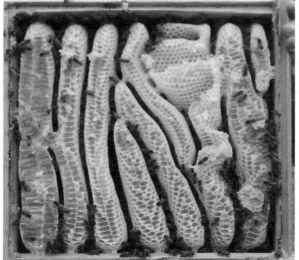

To harvest honey from these boxes I would drum on the box and the bees would run out into the hive.

Working with the box hives taught me a lot about the cycles and natural construction of a wild hive. I experimented with thirty box hives over the course of a year.

After 6 months I was sure they were the answer to all my problems. They are inexpensive to build and easy to construct. I was sold on the idea before I knew if they would be a good long term solution.

By the seventh month I began to see the populations dying off on some of the hives which was a good indicator that many of the hives were swarming. I lost a hive to small hive beetles and while cleaning it up I noticed that the bees were still trying to survive in the hive but they only covered a small portion of the top combs.

The beetles took over the lower combs and were forcing the bees to move up and out. I knew that if this was happening to one hive it was likely to happen to the others. I moved all the other hives over to top bar hives and langstroth hives to avoid the loss and messy cleanup later. During the beetle invasion on my box hives that I endured around this time I had 10 out of 30 hives fly away or slime out. If looking at this experiment from a monetary perspective this was a big loss for me and a lot of extra work.

I choose to look at the educational aspect of this experiment. I now have a greater understanding of comb coverage and swarming behavior. I believe that our role as beekeepers is really all about 'space management'. When a hive fills up it is our time to harvest honey and pollen. When a hive is ready to break their brood cycle and swarm it is our time to catch the swarm or make a split. The rest of the stuff they do all by themselves.

We aid in the management of the beetle drawer. In my bee yards the goal is simplicity. Do it well once so that you do not have to do it again, is my philosophy. I believe that the energy that we put into something is a reflection of what the outcome will be. Enter your hives with intention and commitment to leave it to the bees to know what is best and let them guide you as you go. I never know exactly what I am going to do when I open a hive, I only have a general idea of what may need to be done. It is good to be prepared for everything though so that you do not find yourself without the tools necessary to finish what you started.

For instance, if you were to visit bees that are overflowing out the entrances of their hive and they were full from end to end with combs that were not all straight you may find that the bees may not be all that friendly. If you were to remove a bar and the comb fell off you would want to be sure that you had a bucket ready to put the comb into. I make jokes at my workshops and with my helpers never to open Pandora's box unless you are prepared to find out what is inside. I am not really joking when I say this. I am serious. The bees are the ones who will be greatly effected by messes that are made and not cleaned up. Fallen combs and oozing honey combs could result in a slime out in less than forty-eight hours.

Having foresight is important in all walks of life.

Thinking about every possible scenario and how you may want to perform the required tasks is very helpful before rushing into a possibly messy and painful experience.

I am a fast moving person. I have been told by tall people that they are surprised at how many steps I take compared to theirs and how well I keep up. That fast moving energy is a big similarity that I have with the bees but in the beginning it was also my biggest hurdle to get over.

I was taught some painful lessons about accuracy and patience. I hope to offer you insight in these writings that will save you some of those painful lessons. Most important of all is to 'be here now' when you are in the hive. Do not spend time thinking about your daily life and the many other things that are going on in your world.

When you enter the hive you are in the bees world and it is time to be present with them. Giving them total focus and putting your intention into gathering an understanding of their state of mind is important.

Work through the hive one frame/comb at a time always looking for the queen, eggs, larvae, brood, signs of disease and sickness, honey and pollen stores, queen cups/cells, comb coverage, and pests.

When I first started beekeeping I was so intrigued by the bees and mystified by their nature that I would go and sit with the bees and watch them fly in and out of the hive. I would put my ear up to the side of the hive and listen to them busy working inside. My son started listening to the bees as well and one day he said to me "Mama I hear the queen in there". Sure enough I heard her too. Virgin queens when they emerge from their cells will make a piping sound as they move through the hive.

He could hear the new queen on her victory march. We may form a better connection with bees if we spend time getting to know them a little more and experience them when we are not just there for the honey.

Speaking of honey, it is very sticky. Working with honey is sticky business! Be sure to prepare for your hands being covered with honey and then having to grip a queen and put her in a cage or new hive. That is not always an easy task. Having a bucket of wash water or another source of water is very important.

Here in Hawaii we have honey that comes from the 'ohi'a lehua and kiawe trees that produce solid and creamy honey. Both are delicious but come from very different plants. Kiawe is a relative of mesquite and is an invasive tree that has sharp spikes on it's limbs. The flowers are yellow. The honey from this tree solidifies within twenty-four hours and is white and creamy.

Where we are located we do not have kiawe trees. We have the 'ohi'a lehua trees surrounding all of our apiaries. Several of our apiaries are located at the edge of the Nanawale forest reserve where 'ohi'a trees are numerous. The honey from the lehua flowers also crystalizes in twenty-four to forty-eigth hours. It is important to process these honeys right away. Letting honey sit in a bucket or strainer could cause problems separating the wax from the honey.

When preparing for the bee yard be sure to consider all the possible scenarios so that you will be prepared for them all. Expect to get sticky, stung, hungry, tired, sore, and hot from the sun. Prepare yourself with things that will make those factors less troublesome.

List of supplies for the bee yard:

- 4 buckets for honey, pollen, nectar, and scraps
  (2 extra buckets are needed from honey straining.)
- Sealed container for propolis
- Hive tool
- Brush/feather/hand for removing bees from combs
- Smoker/fuel such as banana leaves and coconut husks, fronds, and fiber
- Lighter
- Staple gun & staples
- Duct tape
- Queen cages
- Rubber bands
- Rags/towels
- Propolis container
- Wash water
- Queen excluder
- Scissors
- Protective wear: hat, veil, gloves, suit
- Extra hive boxes for moving bees and making splits
- Extra frames/bars
- Screwdriver/drill, screws and bits, backup batteries
- Roofing material; always have extra

Above all else is a positive state of mind. What we think creates the outcome of what we do. If you find yourself wondering what you can get your bees to do then you will need to rethink your motives. If you find yourself thinking what could be done here to help the bees then you are on the right track. They know best, just trust and assist.

Multiplying The Apiary or Making Splits

Many people come to my workshops to learn how to split their hives. This is something that can seem intimidating at first. If you follow a few basic steps this process will become much less challenging.

First of all, remember that you can not know what to do until you look and see how the bees are doing. When I first started beekeeping I was given several queens by a beekeeper from Kona. I was so excited to go home and split my hives and use the queens. I read Michael Bush's writings about multiplying hives and I set out to do it that day.

I did not have another yard to move them to so I decided to swap places with the hives so that the new split would be where the old hive was. I also tried to give frames and bees to a caged queen and move them to another area on the farm. Out of six queens that I started with only two survived. The splits that I had moved into the original hive location did well but the ones that I had moved to another location were abandoned by the bees and small hive beetles took over.

I found that some of the hives that the bees did not abscond from had killed the new queen when she came out of her cage and started to raise a new one off of the eggs I had given them in the frames.

Since this time I have developed my own way for making splits in my yards. I am so grateful for the tips I read from another beekeeper and I learned that with small hive beetles there are some new tricks to learn to be successful making splits here. There are many reasons why one may want to split a hive. I split my hives if they are out of room, about to swarm, have mite infestations and are preparing to re-queen, and for genetic diversity.

I will now explain a basic hive inspection and splitting process.

Go slowly and pay attention to detail.

1) Start on the honey side. The opposite end of the entrance.

2) Remove side attachments where the combs touch the wall if needed. Be careful not to pull the comb down as you cut. Cutting upwards with an Italian hive tool or similarly long sharp tool is helpful.

3) As combs are removed **look for the queen**.

As you inspect the combs look at the next combs surface for the queen. Then check the comb that you are inspecting. This is so that if the queen is on the next comb you will not miss her when looking at the one in your hand. Simply place the comb inside the hive and inspect the comb the queen was on. She is often in the brood nest but not always.

4) Check the hive for honey stores and remove all fully capped honey combs. Leave un-capped nectar and brood combs undisturbed.

5) Check for eggs, young larvae, and capped brood.

6) Check for queen cells/cups

If cups or cells are present and have eggs or larva in them then the hive is ready to split.

5) **Find the queen.~**   Do not shake bees or remove brood combs for the split until you find the queen.

5) Once found, cage the queen or place her in a box with a queen excluder over the entrance. If using an excluder make sure that you put the queen on a comb in the new box with bees and close it up carefully. If caging the queen pick her up in your hand and close your hand gently around her.

58

Create an opening with your thumb and
index fingers for her to crawl through. I prefer
to use the JGBG cages available through
beekeeping companies. They have a flip top
with a candy plug.

Once the queen is in the cage you will
add some attendants. This can be tricky.
Grabbing the bees by the wings is a good way to get them into the cage without getting stung. The attendants are helpful but not mandatory.

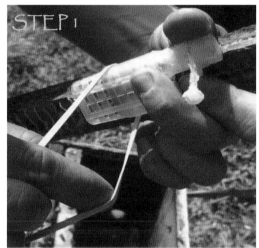

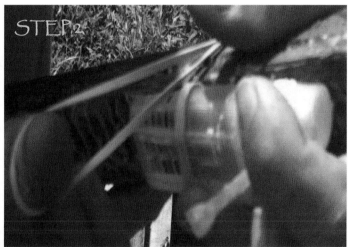

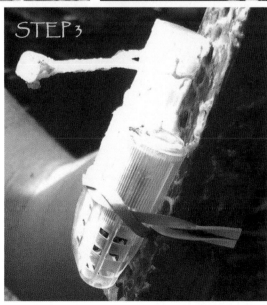

Queen candy is a mixture of honey and powdered sugar. You only need to fill the plug slot with the candy then leave the plug off when you place the cage in the hive. I attach the cage to a frame/top bar with a rubber band.

Once the queen is caged and attached to the frame/bar it is time to shake in the bees and give them a brood comb. Standard practice for me is to make the split with one to three combs of brood and some honey. I do not put full honey combs in a box that I plan to move out of a yard because they are too fragile and could break. When the brood and queen are in place, leave some room on the side by taking out 3-4 bars/frames. Begin shaking in the bees.

This may be challenging at first. It took me time to practice to be able to shake the bees easily. It is really just a flip in the wrist. If you are uncomfortable shaking the bees you may use a feather or fern to remove the bees from the comb. Unless you are using a scale it may be challenging to know when you have 3-5 lbs. of bees. Add more bees as you add more combs for them to cover.

Once you have made the split and closed up the hive place them in the shade until you are ready to transport. When traveling with bees place their frames/bars parallel with the road. This helps to prevent breakage when starting and stopping. Living on cinder roads has been a challenge for me when moving bees. I have to be very careful not to have the combs break when I transport them. Top bar combs are very fragile and may easily break off when transporting. If moving bees in the same yard be sure to move away from the original hive. It is important to get lots of new bees in your split so that you will have adequate support for brood and queen feeding. Foragers are likely to fly back to the original hive until they end their life cycle of 4-6 weeks.

HOW TO BUILD A TOP BAR HIVE

The concept of the top bar hive is to provide honey bees with a safe, natural environment with integrated pest management that allows beekeepers to let bees build and go undisturbed.

The idea for the swarm trap developed after the small hive beetle hit the Big Island of Hawaii. After catching many swarms in the cardboard traps available through bee companies and finding thousands of beetles and their attraction to broken comb, I decided that there must be a better way to catch swarms and transfer them without damaging what they have built and interfering at such a sensitive stage.

If used along with a 36" Top Bar Hive you can have a sustainable way to grow your apiary and encourage bees to reproduce naturally. The best part is that since you do not need to cut combs or remove their combs the bees are safe to grow for one to four weeks in the bait hive before being transferred into the full size hive. Simply move the top bar combs to the new box and shake in the bees. This has simplified my life immensely.

Materials List for 36" T.B. Hive:

- 1" x 12" x 6'   untreated pine, for sides & ends
- 1" x 4" x 8'   untreated pine, for drawer sides & ends
- 1" x 6" x 3'   untreated pine or cedar, for bottom board
  (untreated pine is available in Hilo at HPM (best $) & Home Depot)
- 1/8" metal mesh screen 6" wide x 3' long
  (screen is available in Hilo at Garden Exchange)
- 26 Ea. 1-1/2" Wood Screws
- 10 Ea. 1-1/4"   "
- 8 Ea. 5/8"   "
- 8 Ea. 1/4" x 2" Galv. Carriage Bolts, Nuts, and   Flat Washers
- 40 Approx. 1/2" Staples

Materials List for Swarm Trap:

- 16 Ea. 1-1/2" Wood Screws
- 4 Ea. 1-1/4"   "
- 4 Ea. 5/8"   "
- 14 Approx. 1/2" Staples
- Same size lumber cut to 17" instead of 3'

Assembly:

It is the same process in building the swarm box or the 3' top bar hive. I will include instructions for the full size box.

*THE JIG

If you plan to build top bar hives I recommend starting with the jig. This is fairly straight forward. Start with a 1x12 and mark at 15" from top edge and halfway at 7.5 with a straight edge ruler.

This will give the trapezoidal shape for the follower/divider boards and serve as the jig for building the hive. Attach top bars on the top (15") side of the trapezoid. Be sure to center the jig on the top bar. I recommend making 3 of these to start. One will be your follower board which is used as a false back to the hive when starting a new swarm or nuc.

It is best to use a carpenter's square for measurements and set up of the jig. Place one on each side of the square to set up as shown in the picture on the next page.

• This is the jig set up. The next step is to set the side pieces on the edge of the top bar and rest against the jig. It is important that the jig pieces are the same and that the side pieces are flush against them.

♦ Use small nails to help secure the boards on the edge as you place the side pieces on the jig. The two side pieces are 1" x 12" x 3'.

• Cut two end pieces at 1" x 12" x 17". Rest against the end of the sides and hold in place as you trace the inside of the edges.

• Pre-drill holes in ends and screw onto sides.

It is now time to staple on the screen. Measure the screen to 37.5" long and 7" wide. There will be some overlap but this will help prevent shortage and holes where bees could get in. Place a staple every inch along the inner edge of the wood to secure the screen.

Measure 1" down on both sides edges from the screen. Mark with small nail or pencil line.

Drawer sides are made from 1" x 4" x 3' pine. Pre-drill 4 holes equally spaced along drawer side and frame. Screw on drawer sides. I prefer to screw the sides on from the inside of the hive but you may also screw them on from the outside.

Cut the bottom board to 1" x 6" or 4" x 3'. Attach to the bottom of the drawer sides. I use cedar boards for the bottom because they are less expensive and more resistant to rot and pests. Drawer sides may be cut in shape of drawer or in rectangular pieces. Secure with turn pegs and hinges.

PAINTING

I began painting hives with linseed oil and beeswax but found that it had a tendency to mold. I switched to latex paint and found it weathers similarly. I have started to use translucent stains with 2-3 coats.

Do not paint the inside of the hive.

Leave 1" min. unpainted around the entrances as well.

I have been working with a wonderful hive builder for several years now and I am very pleased with his work. It was important for me to create a sustainable system for others to be able to use for catching swarms and growing their hives. Using the swarm/bait hive to catch swarms and make splits is ideal for moving young hives and allowing them to grow in a more manageable space. For the beginning beekeeper it also makes it less challenging to guide the bees in building

straight combs. These two hives in combination make an easily transferable system that helps bees and beekeepers to grow at their own pace and best manage their space.

There are a few key components to keep in mind when it comes to storing and caring for equipment. In Hawaii we have a wide assortment of insects and pests that are attracted to beekeeping materials. Wax moths, termites, rats, mice, lizards, and cockroaches are just a few of the little critters who may look for shelter in your empty boxes and frames. We also have a very damp environment here where mold is an ongoing issue, especially in the months of November to March. This varies however since we experience many droughts.

Scraping old wax and propolis off the boxes and storing them in a dry area off the ground will help preserve them. If molding occurs use a diluted mix of food grade hydrogen peroxide to wash and sanitize the boxes and frames/bars. Dry in the sun after washing to prevent more molding.

Legs are usually the first part of the hive to rot and need replacement for me. This is problematic because it is the main support for the bees and all their heavy honey. It helps to place the legs on cement or another surface or to cover with more paint if there is no other option. I have resorted to more paint as my solution because my bees are very spread out and surrounded by thick jungle plant life. I maintain the hive areas by cutting back the grass and weeds and I check the hives for needed maintenance and replacement.

I have only needed to recall a few hives this year due to rot and rat damage. Rats chewed through my top bars. In the summer time the hives may need added ventilation so I add bars or rocks under the roof to elevate for wind flow. During the winter months the rats may take refuge under the hive covers and eat away at the bars to create a nest. Limiting access to open spaces will help prevent rat activity.

We also have the little red fire ants here. Unfortunately the only way I have found effective in reducing the populations of these ants is with Amdro. I use small sauce containers with lids and make small ant size holes and store Amdro in them under the hives. I also use a propane torch on equipment and grass surrounding the hive. Keep Amdro and fire away from the bees!!

Catching a Swarm

If you find yourself inspired to catch a swarm one day here are a few tips that might help you along the way.

- Bees rest temporarily in a cluster while scouts search for a new nest. All swarms are different and you have to think quickly but stay calm. Many swarms land on tree branches. Some are easy to remove at low heights and simply shaking them into a new box is all you have to do.

- It may take more than one shake and finding the queen is very important. You may not always find her. Bees may start walking into the box if she is there. Once the bees are in, close it up.

- I give swarms a comb/frame from another hive and a queen excluder over the entrance for 3 days. The excluder keeps the queen in but allows the worker bees to move in & out of the hive freely. The excluder must be removed after 3 days to let the drones out of the hive.

- Some swarms are at more challenging heights. When climbing for a swarm it is good to be prepared. Helpful tools include: rope, bucket with lid, water sprayer (to keep bees from flying), fruit picker (or long stick), honey, lemongrass essential oil, and a clean hive box to move the bees into. You may have to attach the bucket to the stick and use the rope to shake the bees. In some cases you may even cut the branch to remove the bees.

Shake until most bees are in the bucket, then close the lid and lower it down with rope. Once on the ground, shake the bees into their new hive. Look for the queen or bees running in. Watch the tree for activity. Shake until most of the bees are in the hive then place them on a stand near the tree or cluster location. I find that it is best to leave the swarm near the area they clustered at least for a few hours. This attracts other lost bees who got confused during the swarm and allows the bees to settle into their new home. Bees may be moved at night to a new location if necessary. Using a screen or grass plug in their entrance keeps bees from getting out. It is best to place your hive 2 ft. or more off the ground in a sunny area.

Swarms on the east side of Hawaii tend to grow strong very quickly. I began observing a cycle in my bees about a year ago. They grow strong, make lots of bees, produce lots of honey, and then prep for swarming. They tend to begin making queen cells around the sixth week. Many hives would raise five or more queen cells and swarm multiple times.

When bees swarm the old queen flies away with about 75% of the bees in the hive. The remaining bees will stay with the queen cells to maintain the original colony. A virgin queen emerges from her cell ten to twelve days after the egg is placed in the queen cup. She begins piping and exuding her queen scent to attract the bees. An entourage of bees will tend to her and follow her through the hive. An entourage of 5 or more bees is a sign of a healthy queen. The young queens must sting the cells of their rivals, duel it out to the death, or swarm.

The remaining hive will be left with very few bees to defend their combs from small hive beetles. Since the old queen has left there are no eggs in the hive when the new queen is born. This is called a break in their brood cycle. It means that

German queen with entourage

there are no young larvae, only capped brood. When the old brood is born any mites or disease is cleaned up and a new cleaned comb is ready for eggs. This is one of the most common occurrences I experience. This is why I mention it so much throughout these writings. Bees will swarm, it's what they do.

I have two practices for processing honey. I will break them down as crushed comb honey and extracted comb honey.

Crushed comb honey is often from top bar hives or from frames that were not drawn out straight. These are cut off of the bar or frame into a 5 gallon bucket and mashed up with a clean top bar. This is then poured into a strainer bag.

Extracted comb honey is from Langstroth frames. These are processed in a centrifuge extractor. I have been able to reuse extracted foundation-less combs by un-capping them evenly and spinning each side lightly twice. I will only use these

combs for one year and then they will be made into other products. I believe in a no-waste system.

All of the honey goes through a second straining step once it is mashed or spun to remove the wax, propolis, etc. from the honey. This is all poured into a strainer bucket with a spout on it. This makes bottling convenient and easy. The honey is then poured off into buckets or jars and may be stored safely.

Spouts are available through beekeeping companies such as Mann Lake Ltd. I purchased the one in the picture for less than $15. The food grade buckets may be purchased at Home Depot for around $8 for the bucket and lid. You will need a minimum of 4 buckets for this system.

- Bucket #1 is for harvesting and mashing.
- Bucket #2 is for the strainer bucket. Drill lots of holes in this bucket with a 1/8" bit on the bottom. Be sure to remove all pieces of plastic that are lingering. Add a paint strainer bag or straining cloth hanging on the top and this bucket is complete.
- Bucket #3 is for the filtered honey. This is the bottling bucket. Drill or cut a hole to fit the spout. I did this by tracing the spout on the bucket where I wanted to install it and cutting on the inside of the hole to make it a tight fit.
- Bucket #4 is the finished honey bucket. This is best used with a sealed lid and stored in a dry

place until needed. Once opened, honey is at risk of fermentation the more

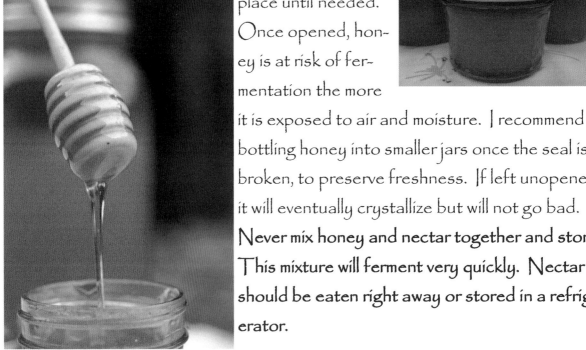

it is exposed to air and moisture. I recommend bottling honey into smaller jars once the seal is broken, to preserve freshness. If left unopened it will eventually crystallize but will not go bad. Never mix honey and nectar together and store. This mixture will ferment very quickly. Nectar should be eaten right away or stored in a refrigerator.

Memorable Lessons From My Teachers

My first teachers of beekeeping were two langstroth hives that I called the 'avo' hive and the 'ulu' hive. When I first introduced myself to them in 2008 they had boxes full of old wax combs and plastic frames. I knew very little then but there was something about those plastic frames that just did not sit well with me.

A friend of mine gave me many files of information about small cell bee-keeping and I read many articles written by Dee Lusby and Michael Bush that made a lot of sense to me. I began removing the plastic frames from the hives one by one by sliding them over to the wall of the hive and waiting for the queen to stop laying eggs in them. After a year I began to see results from doing this. Those hives managed to survive the varroa mites, small hive beetle and *Nosema ceranae* when they hit the island.

It was two years after the pests arrival that the hives began to struggle with chalk brood. I researched chalk brood and consulted with other beekeepers about what they would do in my situation. Many of them told me to re-queen my hives. I bought a queen for the 'avo' hive and replaced the old queen with her. I made a split using the original queen. Both queens laid chalk brood.

I read that it could be the grass around the hive trapping in moisture inside the hive. So I cut the grass and trimmed the trees to allow more sunlight to shine through. Still my teachers were struggling to survive.

I removed all their old combs and forced them to build new combs and their first round of brood was beautiful. No signs of chalk brood at all. The original queen had the same experience. Then by the next cycle of brood I was finding chalk brood and snotbrood. I was at a loss for ideas.

I had been working for another beekeeper at the time for bees and I asked for his advice. He said that because my hives had such high varroa populations they were causing them to have weakened immune systems. He recommended that I use an organically approved miticide called Hopguard to reduce the mite population.

Hesitantly I purchased the Hopguard and I treated three out of four hives on our property. The only hive I did not treat was a top bar nuc that I made with a queen I purchased from a friend. She was kept inside with a queen excluder over the entrance.

Twenty-four hours after I treated the three Langstroth hives I found that my teachers had absconded. The next day the last langstroth hive flew over our heads as we were leaving. I dropped everything and ran for the lemongrass essential oil.

I baited all the swarm boxes and the original hive. The bees reversed direction and flew back towards the original hive but shifted and landed on the top bar nuc. Thousands of bees covered the top bar nuc like a carpet. I contemplated what to do and had some encouragement from my children to take care of it in the morning.

I decided to let the bees figure out what to do and I left. The next morning around 5 a.m. I went out with a two gallon bucket, a brush, and an extra nuc box. I scooped the bees into the bucket and shook them into the empty nuc box.

There was an excluder over the entrance of this hive as well. I did this twice to get as many bees as possible and then I closed the nuc. I carefully removed the top cover and immediately found the queen walking across the top of the bars. I scooped her up in my hand and released her into the new top bar nuc. I scooped up the rest of the bees that were lingering outside of the hive and put them on top of the nuc box.

I opened the original nuc and found the queen and several bees dead on the screen bottom. I put the nuc with the live queen in the place of the original and left them alone for one week. For a long time this was my only hive.

I tell you this story in closing because this was the most monumental moment for me in beekeeping. This experience changed my life forever. I saw bees say "no" to the treatments and choose a different way to live.

I will continue to honor that choice always. My bees have been living examples of evolution and sustainability. I am grateful for their teachings and I am so pleased to be able to share them with others. I am a student of the hive and I know I will continue to have more to share.

Keep your mind open to new possibilities. Let the bees keep you intrigued and always desiring to learn more about their amazing abilities. The more we learn, the more we grow. I am open to all that there is to know.

BEES
ARE
WILD

PARADISE NECTAR APIARIES

LET
THEM
BE

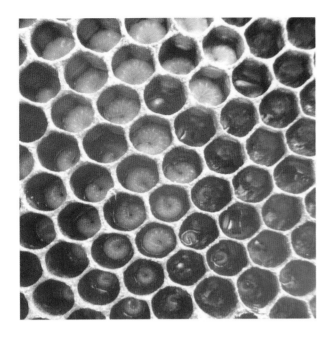

UNCAPPED
WORKER
BROOD

BEES COVERING A
DEAD CENTIPEDE
ON THE BOTTOM
SCREEN.

HONEYBEE
STINGER

LIVE
AS
ONE

THINK
AS
ONE

BEE
AS
ONE

ACKNOWLEDGEMENTS

I would like to start by thanking my wonderful keiki (children) for being so patient with me while compiling this information. I would also like to thank my dear friend and land-mate Ann for her encouragement & inspiration, my ohana (friends & family) for your understanding and support. It is through all of you that I feel the inspiration to teach and share what I have learned.

Mahalo to all of you and may our connections only grow stronger and our intentions be as one like the hive.

As I have mentioned throughout this book I feel it is important to read many books on beekeeping. Reading about what others have tried helps to broaden our understanding of bees and how we may care for them in a healthy way. I am grateful for the beekeepers who have gone before me and who have made their knowledge available. I give thanks for Ed & Dee Lusby for sharing their discoveries of small cell natural beekeeping and inspiring others. Mahalo!

I would like to recommend reading:

"The Practical Beekeeper" by Michael Bush

" Top Bar Beekeeping: Wisdom & Pleasure Combined"
         by Wyatt. Mangum

"The Biology of the Honeybee" by Mark Winston

"The World History of Beekeeping and Honey Hunting" by Eva Crane

"Top Bar Beekeeping" by Les Crowder

"The Barefoot Beekeeper" by P.J. Chandler

"The Shamanic Way of the Bee" by Simon Buxton

There are many other books about beekeeping that I could list.

These are some of my favorites. Enjoy!

GLOSSARY & INDEX

Made in the USA
Charleston, SC
28 May 2015